MAKING MONEY ONLINE: BOOK 1

BY MICHAEL CALLUM MAYAKA

Second Edition
Brought to you by MCM Publications (books.michaelmayaka.co.uk)

UNDERSTANDING THE ONLINE LANDSCAPE

FOREWORD:

In today's digital age, making money online has become a viable and accessible option for individuals seeking financial independence or additional income streams. The internet offers a plethora of opportunities that allow you to leverage your skills, creativity, and resources to generate revenue. This guide aims to provide you with valuable insights, strategies, and practical tips on how to make money online effectively.

This book is part of a series for more information see Further reading at the end of this book.

Table of Contents

Foreword: 4
1. Understanding the Online Landscape 6
    1.1 The Evolution of Online Income Opportunities 7
        1. E-commerce and Online Retail: 8
        2. Freelancing and Remote Work: 9
        3. Content Creation and Monetization: 9
        4. Online Tutoring and Education: 10
        5. Online Surveys, Microtasks, and Rewards: 11
        6. Online Investments and Trading: 12
    1.2 Benefits and Challenges of Making Money Online 14
        Benefits: 15
        Challenges: 19
    1.3 Essential Skills and Mindset for Online Success 23
Further reading: 31

1. UNDERSTANDING THE ONLINE LANDSCAPE

1.1 THE EVOLUTION OF ONLINE INCOME OPPORTUNITIES

In recent years, the internet has revolutionized the way we live, work, and make money. With the rapid advancement of technology and the widespread accessibility of the internet, a multitude of online income opportunities have emerged. Let's explore the evolution of these opportunities and how they have transformed the way individuals earn a living.

1. E-COMMERCE AND ONLINE RETAIL:

The rise of e-commerce platforms, such as Amazon and eBay, has opened up new avenues for entrepreneurs and small businesses to sell products online. With the ability to reach a global customer base and the convenience of dropshipping, individuals can set up their own online stores with relative ease. Additionally, the emergence of digital products, such as e-books and online courses, has further expanded the potential for generating revenue in the e-commerce realm.

2. FREELANCING AND REMOTE WORK:

The gig economy has flourished with the advent of online freelancing platforms like Upwork, Freelancer, and Fiverr. These platforms connect freelancers with clients seeking specific skills, ranging from graphic design and writing to programming and virtual assistance. Remote work has become increasingly popular, allowing individuals to work from anywhere in the world and collaborate with clients and teams globally.

3. CONTENT CREATION AND MONETIZATION:

The rise of social media platforms and streaming services has created a new breed of online entrepreneurs - content creators. Platforms like YouTube, Instagram, and TikTok have provided individuals with the opportunity to showcase their creativity, entertain audiences, and monetize their content through advertising, brand partnerships, and sponsorships. Additionally, blogging and podcasting have gained traction, allowing individuals to share their expertise, build an audience, and earn revenue through advertising, affiliate marketing, and sponsored content.

4. ONLINE TUTORING AND EDUCATION:

The internet has transformed the education industry, enabling individuals to offer tutoring and educational services online. Virtual tutoring platforms like VIPKid and iTalki connect language learners with tutors worldwide. Moreover, the rise of e-learning platforms, such as Udemy and Coursera, has made it possible for instructors to create and sell online courses on a wide range of subjects.

5. ONLINE SURVEYS, MICROTASKS, AND REWARDS:

For those looking to earn smaller amounts of money or rewards, online surveys, microtasks, and rewards programs provide opportunities to make money online. Websites and apps offer paid surveys, where users can provide feedback and opinions in exchange for cash or gift cards. Microtask platforms, such as Amazon Mechanical Turk, allow individuals to complete small tasks for a fee. Additionally, cashback and rewards programs incentivize online shopping by offering cashback, discounts, or loyalty points.

6. ONLINE INVESTMENTS AND TRADING:

The digital era has also opened up avenues for online investments and trading. With online brokerage platforms, individuals can easily invest in stocks, bonds, and other financial instruments. Furthermore, the emergence of cryptocurrencies and cryptocurrency exchanges has created opportunities for individuals to trade and invest in digital assets.

The evolution of online income opportunities has provided individuals with unprecedented flexibility, scalability, and global reach. However, it is important to note that success in the online realm requires dedication, hard work, and continuous learning. With the right skills, mindset, and willingness to adapt to changing trends, individuals can tap into the vast potential of making money online.

1.2 BENEFITS AND CHALLENGES OF MAKING MONEY ONLINE

Making money online has become increasingly popular and offers numerous benefits, as well as certain challenges that aspiring online entrepreneurs should be aware of. Understanding both sides of the coin is essential for anyone looking to embark on an online money-making journey. In this section, we will discuss the benefits and challenges of making money online.

BENEFITS:

1. Flexibility and Convenience: One of the most significant advantages of making money online is the flexibility it provides. You have the freedom to work from anywhere, be it your home, a coffee shop, or while traveling. Additionally, you can set your own schedule, allowing you to balance work with personal commitments or other responsibilities.

2. Diverse Income Opportunities: The internet offers a vast array of income opportunities. Whether you're interested in e-commerce, freelancing, content creation, online tutoring, or consulting, there is a niche for almost every skill set or passion.

This variety allows you to explore different avenues and find the one that aligns best with your interests and expertise.

3. Low Startup Costs: Many online business models require minimal upfront investment compared to traditional brick-and-mortar ventures. For instance, starting an e-commerce store can be done with a relatively low budget by utilizing dropshipping or print-on-demand services. Blogging or creating digital products often requires only a domain name, hosting, and some software tools, making it accessible to a wide range of individuals.

4. Global Reach and Market Access: The internet breaks down geographical barriers, enabling you to reach a global audience. With the right marketing strategies and online platforms, you can sell products or services to customers worldwide, expanding your market reach beyond local boundaries. This opens up immense growth opportunities and the potential for higher earnings.

5. Scalability and Passive Income Potential: Online businesses have the advantage of scalability. Once you establish a successful online venture, such as an e-commerce store, a popular blog, or a digital product, you can scale it up to reach a larger audience and generate more revenue. Furthermore,

some online income streams, such as affiliate marketing or selling digital products, have the potential to generate passive income, where you earn money even when you're not actively working.

CHALLENGES:

1. Self-Discipline and Time Management: Working online requires self-discipline and effective time management skills. With no strict office hours or a supervisor, it's easy to become distracted or procrastinate. Maintaining focus and establishing a routine are crucial to stay productive and achieve your income goals.

2. Market Saturation and Competition: The online marketplace can be highly competitive, especially in popular niches. It may take time and effort to stand out from the crowd and build a significant customer base. Thorough market research, a unique selling proposition, and consistent quality

are essential to overcome the challenges posed by competition.

3. Technical Skills and Learning Curve: Many online money-making methods involve a learning curve and the need to acquire new technical skills. Whether it's setting up a website, learning digital marketing techniques, or understanding analytics, there is a continuous need for self-education and staying up-to-date with evolving technologies.

4. Online Security and Scams: The online world also presents security risks, including scams and frauds. It's essential to be cautious and take necessary precautions to

protect your personal information, financial transactions, and online reputation. Conduct thorough research, use secure payment gateways, and be wary of suspicious offers or requests.

5. Income Volatility and Uncertainty: Online income can be subject to volatility, especially in the early stages. It may take time to establish a steady flow of revenue, and income levels can fluctuate. Adapting to changing market conditions, diversifying income streams, and building a financial safety net are essential to manage income uncertainty effectively.

By understanding the benefits and challenges of making money online, you can approach your online ventures with realistic expectations and a prepared mindset. With perseverance, determination, and a willingness to learn, you can navigate the challenges and leverage the benefits to build a successful and rewarding online income stream.

1.3 ESSENTIAL SKILLS AND MINDSET FOR ONLINE SUCCESS

In the fast-paced and ever-evolving world of making money online, certain skills and a specific mindset can significantly contribute to your success. While the digital landscape offers countless opportunities, it also demands certain capabilities and qualities to thrive in this competitive space. Let's explore some essential skills and the right mindset required for online success.

1. Self-Discipline: Online endeavours often provide flexibility, allowing you to work on your own terms. However, this freedom can be a double-edged sword. Without self-

discipline, it's easy to succumb to distractions and procrastination. Developing a structured work routine, setting achievable goals, and maintaining focus are crucial for consistent progress and productivity.

2. Adaptability and Continuous Learning: The online landscape is dynamic, with trends and technologies constantly evolving. To stay relevant and ahead of the curve, it's vital to embrace change and continuously update your skills. Be open to learning new tools, platforms, and strategies, as this will enable you to adapt to market shifts and capitalize on emerging opportunities.

3. Strong Communication Skills: Effective communication is essential in the digital realm, where interactions often occur remotely and rely heavily on written or virtual communication channels. Honing your written and verbal communication skills will enhance your ability to connect with clients, customers, and collaborators. Clear and concise communication can foster trust, build relationships, and lead to successful collaborations.

4. Digital Literacy: Developing a strong foundation in digital literacy is crucial for online success. Familiarize yourself with various digital tools, software, and

platforms relevant to your chosen online field. This includes proficiency in using productivity tools, content management systems, analytics platforms, and social media channels. Being technologically savvy will enable you to navigate the online world efficiently and leverage available resources effectively.

5. Marketing and Branding Skills: In a crowded online marketplace, standing out and attracting an audience is vital. Understanding the fundamentals of marketing and branding is key to building your online presence and reaching your target audience. Learn about effective marketing strategies, search engine optimization (SEO), social media

marketing, and content creation. Craft a compelling personal brand that reflects your expertise and values, and consistently promote yourself across relevant channels.

6. Problem-Solving and Critical Thinking: Online endeavours often present challenges and obstacles. Developing strong problem-solving and critical thinking skills will help you overcome hurdles and find innovative solutions. Embrace a proactive and solution-oriented mindset, and view obstacles as opportunities for growth. Analyze problems from different angles, explore alternative approaches, and leverage your creativity to find unique solutions.

7. Resilience and Persistence: Making money online can be a rollercoaster ride, with ups and downs along the way. It's crucial to develop resilience and persistence to navigate setbacks and failures. Understand that success may not come overnight, and setbacks are valuable learning experiences. Maintain a positive mindset, embrace failures as stepping stones, and keep pushing forward with determination and resilience.

8. Networking and Collaboration: Building a strong network and fostering collaborations can open doors to new opportunities and accelerate your online success. Engage with like-minded individuals, participate in online

communities and forums, attend virtual conferences and webinars, and actively seek collaborations. Networking can lead to partnerships, mentorship opportunities, and access to valuable resources and knowledge.

In conclusion, cultivating essential skills and adopting the right mindset are pivotal for online success. Develop self-discipline, adaptability, strong communication skills, digital literacy, marketing acumen, problem-solving abilities, resilience, and a proactive networking approach. Combine these skills with a growth mindset, passion for learning, and a commitment to excellence. With these attributes, you'll be well-equipped to navigate the online landscape, seize opportunities, and achieve your financial goals.

FURTHER READING:

If you enjoyed this book, please consider reading one of the other books in the series:

Making Money Online: Book 1 (Understanding the Online Landscape)

Making Money Online: Book 2 (E-commerce and Online Retail)

Making Money Online: Book 3 (Freelancing and Remote Work)

Making Money Online: Book 4 (Content Creation and Monetization)

Making Money Online: Book 5 (Online Tutoring and Education)

Making Money Online: Book 6 (Online Surveys, Microtasks, and Rewards)

Making Money Online: Book 7 (Online Investments and Trading)

Making Money Online: Book 8 (Creating and Selling Digital Assets)

Making Money Online: Book 9 (Online Consulting and Coaching)

Making Money Online: Book 10 (Maximizing Online Income Opportunities)

All the books can be found on Amazon as Kindle and Paperback, or you can buy the complete edition which contains the full series in one book. The complete edition is available as Kindle, Paperback and exclusively as Hardback. You can find all the links in my book site: books.michaelmayaka.co.uk.

Use the following space to make your own notes:

www.ingramcontent.com/pod-product-compliance
Lightning Source LLC
Chambersburg PA
CBHW040259220526
45473CB00002B/535